Adorable Akitas

A COLOURING BOOK FOR ADULTS

Paws for Thought: Vol. 16

Christine Vencato

This book is dedicated to my wonderful family

Illustrations and design © 2019 Christine Vencato

www.arttherapycolouringbook.org

First edition; first printing

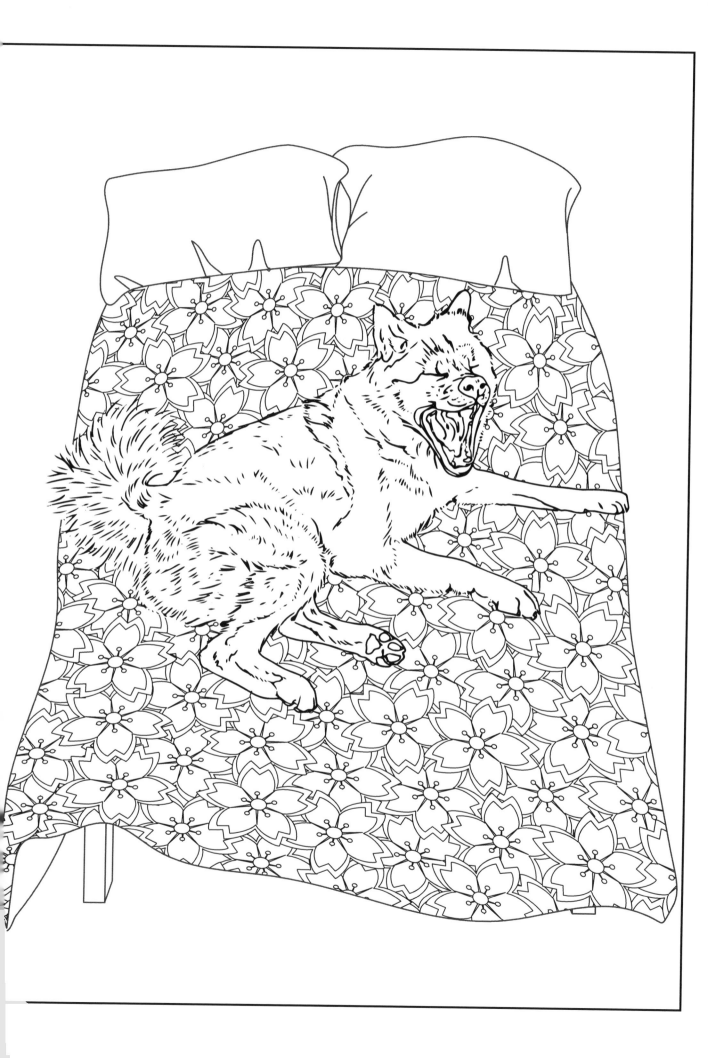

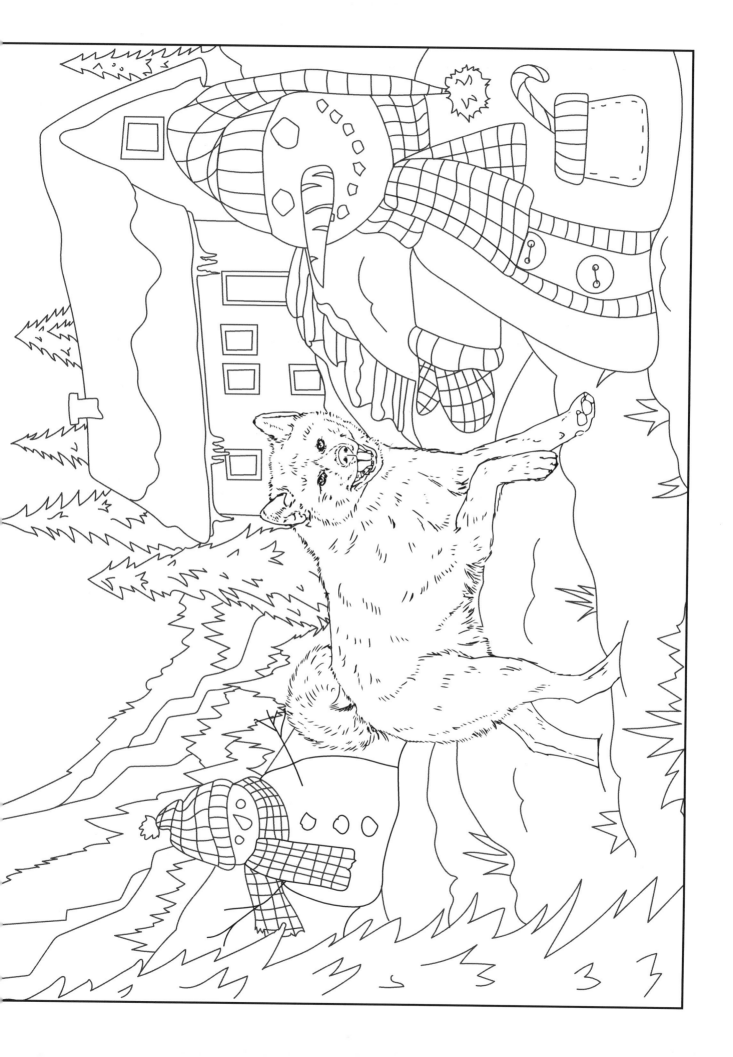

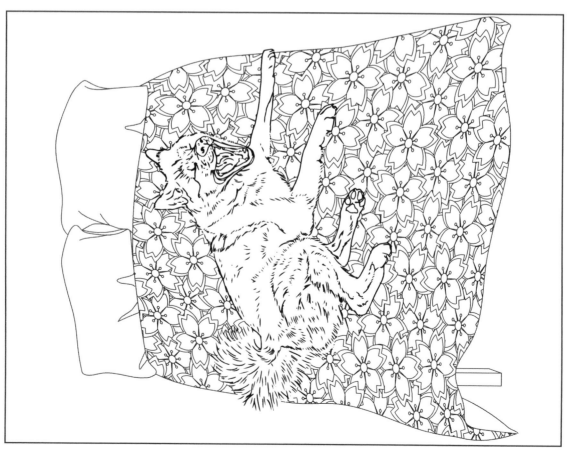

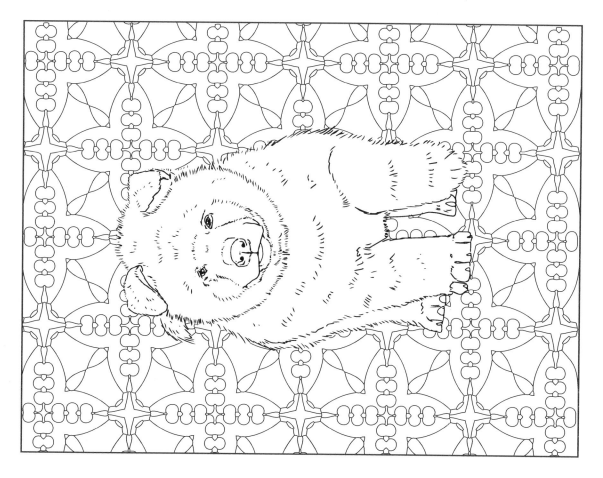